CW01425606

Copyright © 1982 Editions Duculot, Paris-Gembloux
First published in Belgium
under the title *Le Patchwork*
All rights reserved
First published in Great Britain 1986 by
Julia MacRae Books
A division of Franklin Watts
12a Golden Square, London, W1R 4BA
and Franklin Watts Australia
14 Mars Road, Lane Cove, NSW 2066

Vincent, G
Ernest and Celestine's patchwork quilt.
I. Title II. Le patchwork. *English*
843'.914[J]   PZ7
ISBN 0-86203-281-4
Printed in Belgium

Gabrielle Vincent

ERNEST
AND
CELESTINE'S
PATCHWORK
QUILT

Julia MacRae Books

A DIVISION OF FRANKLIN WATTS